Original title:
A New Song

Copyright © 2024 Swan Charm
All rights reserved.

Author: Eliora Lumiste
ISBN HARDBACK: 978-9916-89-757-7
ISBN PAPERBACK: 978-9916-89-758-4
ISBN EBOOK: 978-9916-89-759-1

Soliloquy of Wonder

In the stillness of the night,
Heaven whispers soft delight,
Stars above, a sacred sign,
In this heart, your love I find.

Touch the earth with gentle grace,
Guide my steps in this vast space,
Every breath, a prayer sent high,
In your presence, I rely.

Questions linger, doubts may swirl,
Yet your light in darkness twirls,
With each moment, truth unfolds,
In the quiet, hope consoled.

Nature sings a hymn so sweet,
In the silence, feel the beat,
All creation sings your praise,
Through my heart, your glory stays.

Let my soul, a canvas bare,
Paint your name in every prayer,
In the wonder, I will dwell,
In your love, I find my shell.

A Canvas of Sacred Sounds

In the dawn, the choir sings,
Heartstrings pulled by sacred wings,
Every note, a gift divine,
Crafting peace in every line.

With the wind, your whispers flow,
Bringing warmth to us below,
Nature hums a holy tune,
Guiding hearts to meet the moon.

In the echoes of the night,
Find the path that leads to light,
Each refrain, a step we take,
In this bond, no hearts will break.

Harmony in every breath,
Life and love, defying death,
In this rhythm, we unite,
Finding strength in shared insight.

On this canvas, paint my soul,
With your love, I am made whole,
Each sound, a thread in the seam,
Weaving joy, a sacred dream.

The Music of Faith's Echo

In the quiet, faith resounds,
In the heart, your love abounds,
Every prayer, a gentle sigh,
In your grace, I learn to fly.

Through the trials, you are near,
With each tear, you wipe my fear,
Songs of hope in struggle rise,
In your mercy, I am wise.

Every challenge, gift in guise,
Lift me up to heaven's skies,
With your strength, I walk the road,
Grateful, I share this load.

In the whispers of the night,
Feel your presence, pure and bright,
Music flows and fills the space,
In your love, I find my place.

Let my heart be tuned to you,
In this dance, the old, the new,
Each echo speaks your name with pride,
In this faith, I shall abide.

Crescendo of the Devout

From the shadows, light will break,
Every heart begins to wake,
In the stillness, voices rise,
Harmonies that seek the skies.

Gathered 'round in prayerful peace,
Hope and love shall never cease,
With each note, a promise clear,
In our faith, we draw you near.

Mountains high and valleys low,
In our souls, your love will flow,
Crescendo of the devout,
In your grace, we live it out.

As the sun begins to rise,
Sing our truths, we touch the skies,
Every heartbeat, sacred sound,
In your mercy, we are found.

Let our offerings be sincere,
In your presence, feel you near,
With our voices, we proclaim,
All our lives, we praise your name.

The Rebirth of Sacred Chords

In twilight's grace, the echoes rise,
With voices soft, they touch the skies.
A harmony reborn in light,
Guiding souls through the endless night.

The ancient hymns, a sacred flow,
Chanting truth that all may know.
As hearts awaken, spirits soar,
The chords of faith forever more.

With every note, a promise made,
A tapestry of love displayed.
In unity, we find our place,
Embraced within divine embrace.

In silence found, we seek the sound,
In every prayer, a love unbound.
The sacred chain that holds us tight,
Transcending darkness, bringing light.

Renewed in spirit, we unite,
With sacred chords, our hearts ignite.
A symphony of purest grace,
In every life, the truth we trace.

Celestial Resonance

Beneath the stars, the heavens sing,
In cosmic dance, our spirits cling.
A resonance that fills the night,
In every heart a spark of light.

The whispers soft of distant skies,
In infinite realms, our love shall rise.
Each note a wave of hope bestowed,
A path of faith, a sacred road.

With every breath, we seek His face,
In tender arms, we find our place.
The harmony that lights our way,
In joyous songs, we rise and sway.

In unity, our voices blend,
Through trials faced, the light will mend.
For every tear, a chord will hold,
A story of love eternally told.

Let every heart a beacon be,
In celestial tunes, we find our plea.
With faith's embrace, we'll ever sing,
A melody of life's offering.

Graceful Melodies of Hope

In gentle tones, the morning glows,
As grace unfolds, our spirit grows.
Each moment blessed, a gift divine,
A melody of hope, a sacred sign.

In whispered prayers, the heart does plead,
Through trials faced, we plant the seed.
With every song, a dream takes flight,
In faith's embrace, we seek the light.

The symphony of life rolls on,
In every loss, new strength is drawn.
We rise anew, our hearts so pure,
In faith's embrace, we shall endure.

With joyful hearts, we sing as one,
In every journey, love is spun.
Graceful melodies fill the air,
With hope's sweet song, we find our prayer.

So gather 'round, let voices blend,
In smiling hearts, the love will mend.
A resonant truth, forever clear,
In harmony, we cast out fear.

The Spirit's Lament in Sunrise

As dawn breaks forth, the world awakes,
In gentle sighs, the spirit aches.
A lament heard in morning's light,
In shadows deep, we seek His might.

The golden rays, a tender touch,
In whispered dreams, we long for much.
As day unfolds its vibrant hue,
Our spirits yearn to be made new.

With every breath, a prayer ascends,
In sacred silence, the soul transcends.
The promise held in each sunrise,
In every tear, a hope that lies.

Through trials faced and hearts laid bare,
In faith's embrace, we find our care.
For every sorrow, love will rise,
In quiet moments, we touch the skies.

In every dawn, a chance to see,
The spirit's path, forever free.
In unity, our hearts are one,
Embraced by grace, our fears undone.

Reverence in Every Note

In the silence, whispers dwell,
Every heartbeat sings a spell.
Spirit guides our fervent prayers,
In the stillness, love declares.

As the dawn brings light anew,
In our hearts, hope breaks through.
Melodies of grace resound,
In each note, peace is found.

Humbled souls, we stand in awe,
Yearning for a deeper law.
With each hymn, we lift our gaze,
To the heavens, purest praise.

Through the trials, we remain,
Holding fast, though faced with pain.
In the echo of our song,
Love and faith will guide us on.

The Chorus of Sacred Beginnings

In the quiet, voices blend,
Songs of old, our hearts transcend.
With each note, a promise made,
In the light, fears shall fade.

Children of the dawn arise,
With joy bright, we seek the skies.
Life renewed in reverence,
Singing forth ourfound essence.

As the stars begin to gleam,
We become the waking dream.
Every breath, a chance to start,
Harmony within the heart.

Together hand in hand, we stand,
A united faith so grand.
Through the darkness, we will shine,
In the love, pure and divine.

Canticles of the Reborn Spirit

In shadows deep, a light shall rise,
Awakening the darkest skies.
Voices call, a gentle plea,
Transcending time, setting free.

With every step, the path unfolds,
Stories whispered, truths retold.
In each tear, a lesson learned,
By the fire, our spirits burned.

Witness now the sacred tide,
Washing over, hearts abide.
Breath of life, our souls ignite,
In this love, we seek the light.

With open arms, we shall embrace,
All creation, share this space.
United in this holy hymn,
Life anew, our hopes begin.

Lullabies of Faith's Embrace

In the stillness, cradled tight,
Whisper soft, the stars ignite.
Through the night, our dreams take flight,
Guided by the sacred light.

Every heartbeat, a gentle song,
In this love, we all belong.
Rest your fears, let go of strife,
In His arms, we find our life.

As the moon casts silver rays,
Warming souls in tender displays.
Echoes of faith softly weave,
In this peace, we all believe.

And as daylight breaks the dawn,
With hope renewed, our spirits drawn.
We rise anew, in love's embrace,
Faith will lead us, we find grace.

Revelations in the Stillness

In the quietude of the night,
Whispers of wisdom take flight.
Stars above like candles aglow,
Illuminating pathways below.

Breathe in the silence, breathe deep,
Across the vastness, secrets seep.
The heart listens, a vessel of grace,
In stillness, we seek the sacred space.

Nature speaks in a soothing hush,
In every rustle, in every rush.
Moments of pause, divine and rare,
Unveiling truths beyond compare.

Mountains resonate with ancient calls,
Echoes of faith in the forest's thralls.
From humble stones to celestial skies,
In stillness, the eternal ties.

Awake, arise, to the gentle embrace,
Of revelations found in solace.
In the stillness, seek and find,
The whispers of the soul entwined.

Harmonies from the Eternal Well

From depths divine, a melody flows,
Through sacred waters, the spirit knows.
Each note, a prayer that softly swells,
In deep connection, the heart compels.

Rippling echoes of pure delight,
The dawn of grace in soft twilight.
Each harmony, a soul's refrain,
In the dance of life, joy in the pain.

Stars align in symphonic light,
A chorus rising in the night.
Harmony sings of the great design,
In unity found, the heart's entwine.

With every breath, the verses spin,
Life unfolds where we begin.
In the rhythm of love, we dwell,
Embraced by grace from the eternal well.

Let us listen, let us sing,
In every moment, the joy we bring.
For in the echoes, true magic lies,
In harmonies born from the skies.

A Symphony of Grace

With each sunrise, a symphony starts,
Building the rhythm of grateful hearts.
Nature's orchestra, a sacred play,
Guiding our steps along the way.

Birds in chorus, leaves in dance,
Every moment, a second chance.
In joy and sorrow, grace arrives,
In the music of life, the spirit thrives.

Notes of kindness, chords of love,
Flowing gently from above.
Through trials and triumphs, we are blessed,
Breath by breath, a divine quest.

Recognize the beauty in every face,
Life awakens in the arms of grace.
In the symphony of the heart's refrain,
Love's melody will forever remain.

Together we rise, together we soar,
In unity found, we are more.
In each moment, a chance to embrace,
The everlasting gift of grace.

The Song of Transcendence

In the shadow of mountains high,
Whispers of love dance and sigh.
Transcendence calls from the depths of night,
Inviting hearts to the source of light.

Through trials faced, we find our wings,
In the silence, the spirit sings.
Emerging strong from pain's embrace,
In the realm of hope, we find our place.

Golden rays of dawn unfold,
Stories of faith gently told.
Awake the soul, let the journey start,
In the song of life, we play our part.

With every note, the heart ignites,
Transcendence found in endless flights.
Over valleys deep and oceans wide,
In the eternal song, we abide.

Embrace the journey, let go the fear,
In the symphony, we draw near.
The song of transcendence ever sings,
A melody rich with eternal things.

A Tapestry of Graceful Echoes

In the stillness of dawn's embrace,
Whispers of mercy fill the air,
Threads of hope woven with grace,
Guiding souls, hearts laid bare.

Light cascades from heavens above,
Illuminating paths once dark,
Each step, a dance of sacred love,
In every shadow, faith must spark.

Voices rise like gentle streams,
Carrying prayers beyond the skies,
In unity, we stitch our dreams,
With hands uplifted, spirits rise.

Nature sings her sweet refrain,
Mountains echo the heartbeat's song,
In every joy, in every pain,
In the tapestry, we belong.

As twilight wraps the world in grace,
We gather, hearts entwined as one,
In divine presence, we find our place,
Embraced by love's eternal sun.

Echoes of Praise in the Twilight

As day gives way to evening's glow,
Our voices lift in joyful song,
In the dusk, the spirits flow,
Echoes of praise where we belong.

Each note a whisper of the heart,
Resonating through the night,
In the silence, we take part,
In the warmth of His guiding light.

Stars awaken, the heavens gleam,
A celestial choir sings along,
In unity, we weave our dream,
Hearts aligned, our love is strong.

With every echo, we are found,
Rooted deep in grace profound,
In the twilight, our souls abound,
In every moment, sacred ground.

So let the night be filled with praise,
As we journey through the divine,
In whispers soft, and spirits blaze,
Together, our hearts intertwine.

The Tranquil Reverberation of Faith

In the quietude of morning's light,
Faith like a river flows so wide,
Each drop a promise, pure and bright,
In every heart, His love abides.

Through valley lows and mountain highs,
The echoes of trust steady our way,
In the storms, His presence lies,
A beacon for us, come what may.

Every prayer a gentle breeze,
Whispers dancing in softest tunes,
In stillness, the spirit frees,
Calling us closer, under the moons.

Life unfolds in sacred grace,
With each breath, the sacred sings,
In every challenge, we embrace,
The tranquil joy that faith brings.

Our hearts united, we will stand,
As echoes blend in harmony,
Hand in hand, guided by His hand,
In the fabric of divinity.

Awakening with Every Breath

With every breath, we rise anew,
As dawn awakens the day,
In gratitude, our spirits grew,
Caressed by light in gentle play.

Each moment a chance to reflect,
In harmony, we find our way,
In divine love, we reconnect,
What is woven cannot fray.

Nature hums a soothing tune,
As colors blend in vibrant swirls,
In the stillness, hearts commune,
With sacred whispers, joy unfurls.

Together we seek, forever true,
In the rhythm of life divine,
Awakening, as love breaks through,
In every heartbeat, He does shine.

So let us breathe, let us embrace,
The sacred dance we all partake,
In a world adorned with grace,
United in the love we make.

Prayerful Resonation

In quiet whispers, I ascend,
To realms where spirit meets the sky.
Each prayer a thread, a sacred blend,
In faith's embrace, the soul will fly.

With every heartbeat, hope's refrain,
A melody of trust and light.
The burdens lift, released from pain,
In love's embrace, we find our sight.

In shadows cast by doubt and fear,
I call upon the strength within.
The sacred voice is always near,
Guiding me back to grace again.

Through trials faced, I learn to see,
The blessings woven in the strife.
In prayerful moments, I am free,
To find the joy, to taste the life.

With every breath, a praise is sung,
An anthem for the broken soul.
In unity, our songs are flung,
To bind us whole, to make us whole.

Chorus of the Believing Heart

In humble tones, our voices rise,
A chorus of the purest light.
With open hearts and lifted eyes,
We seek the truth, embrace the right.

Each soul a note in harmony,
Together forming sacred sound.
In love's embrace, we long to be,
Where peace and grace are fully found.

Through trials faced, we stand as one,
In faith's strong hold, we find our way.
The journey long, the race not run,
But with each step, we choose to pray.

In every word, a promise glows,
A beacon in the darkest night.
The chorus grows as courage flows,
In believing hearts, we find the light.

Together we will walk this path,
As one united, strong and free.
In joyous song, we face the wrath,
With hope and trust in unity.

The Symphony of Graceful Return

In silence deep, we seek to find,
A symphony of love so rare.
Each note a grace, entwined and kind,
In every heartbeat, tender prayer.

The journey long, yet sweet the call,
With faith as guide, we find our way.
The echoes of the love enthrall,
In grace we live, in truth we stay.

Through valleys low, to mountains high,
We walk together, hand in hand.
With every sigh, we learn to fly,
In harmony, our hearts expand.

The lessons learned, the tears we've shed,
In every trial, wisdom grows.
With open hearts, no words unsaid,
In symphony, our spirit flows.

The grace of love will bring us home,
A journey shared, forever true.
In unity, no need to roam,
The symphony of us breaks through.

The Celestial Overture

From heavens high, the stars proclaim,
A celestial song that guides our way.
In every heart, a sacred flame,
The overture of night and day.

With gentle whispers, spirits soar,
In cosmic dance, we find our peace.
Each heartbeat echoes love's deep roar,
In unity, our fears release.

Beneath the sky, a tapestry,
In starlit dreams, we find our path.
The beauty lies in harmony,
In joy and pain, we share the wrath.

Through trials faced, we rise anew,
In grace bestowed, our spirits sing.
The overture forever true,
Awakens hope in everything.

In perfect time, we find our place,
A dance of life that never ends.
In every moment, find His grace,
The celestial song forever blends.

The Celestial Anthem

In the stillness of the night,
Soft whispers reach the sky,
Angels sing of love so bright,
Heaven's grace will never die.

Stars align in purest praise,
Guiding hearts to holy light,
Each soul finds its sacred ways,
In the silence, trust takes flight.

Mountains echo, valleys hum,
Nature's voice, a sacred song,
In the rhythm, we become,
Part of all, we all belong.

Through the storms, we seek the calm,
Faith and hope our steadfast guide,
In His arms, we find the balm,
A celestial love inside.

Let us lift our voices high,
United in the sacred call,
Together reaching for the sky,
In the anthem, we stand tall.

Sacred Voices of the Night

Underneath the moon's soft glow,
Whispers dance upon the breeze,
Ancient words of love we know,
In the shadows, spirits tease.

Silent prayers rise like the mist,
Carried forth by gentle sighs,
In each moment, love persists,
As the sacred night complies.

Stars are eyes of those above,
Watching over, bright and clear,
Every twinkling spark is love,
Calling all who want to hear.

In the stillness, hearts unite,
Bound by faith, both near and far,
Guided by the blessed light,
Walking pathways marked by stars.

Let us gather, souls ablaze,
Find our peace in twilight's glow,
In this sacred, endless phase,
Voices rise, a love we know.

The Symphony of Hope Unfurled

In the dawn where shadows fade,
Hope arises, strong and bright,
Every heart, a note well played,
Weaving songs of pure delight.

Through the trials that we face,
Melodies of courage soar,
In the struggle, find our place,
Harmony forevermore.

Softly, gently spirits sing,
Lifting weary souls anew,
Grace and faith, the offering,
All is possible and true.

Let the symphony resound,
Echoing through every land,
In our hearts, the love is found,
Joined together, hand in hand.

With each note, the world transforms,
In the light of hope we trust,
Through the calm and raging storms,
In the music, rise we must.

Reverberations from the Holy

In the stillness, whispers rise,
Echoes of the divine grace,
Touching hearts, revealing ties,
In the silence, we embrace.

Mountains tremble, waters flow,
Nature speaks in sacred tones,
In the songs of winds that blow,
We find refuge, no more bones.

Every dawn, a new refrain,
Painting skies with love's embrace,
In the joy and also pain,
We remember our true place.

With each heartbeat, prayers unfold,
Stories woven into time,
In the quiet, trust is bold,
Life's sweet melody, a rhyme.

So let the reverberate sound,
Travel far beyond the night,
In each moment, love is found,
In the holy, we find light.

Harmonies Forged in Prayer

In silence deep, our spirits weave,
A melody that hearts believe.
With whispered hopes, and voices raised,
In faith's embrace, our souls are praised.

With every word, a bond is formed,
In humble hearts, the love is warmed.
For in the struggle, grace does flow,
In prayerful nights, our spirits grow.

Through trials faced, we find our strength,
In unity, we go the length.
Each heartbeat echoes heaven's call,
Together we stand, we shall not fall.

In sacred spaces, hands unite,
A circle strong, in purest light.
With every tear, a blessing flows,
In prayerful hearts, true love bestows.

So let us sing, our voices high,
In harmony, we touch the sky.
For every prayer, a note so pure,
In faith's embrace, our souls endure.

A Chorus of Radiant Hearts

Beneath the stars, our spirits soar,
In radiant love, we seek much more.
With every song, a light ignites,
A chorus strong, through darkest nights.

In gentle whispers, kindness blooms,
With open hearts, dispelling glooms.
Together we rise, a faithful band,
In unity's grip, we make our stand.

With hands outstretched, we bridge the gap,
In every heart, a sacred map.
With faith as anchor, we will find,
A radiant path, where love is blind.

As sun breaks through the morning mist,
In every soul, a promised tryst.
Through trials faced, our spirits gleam,
In faith's embrace, we are redeemed.

So let us sing, a song of hope,
In every note, learn how to cope.
With radiant hearts, we shall proclaim,
In joyous love, we share His name.

Tones of the Faithful Pilgrim

With weary feet, we walk the road,
Each step in faith, our burdens owed.
Through valleys low and mountains high,
In every tear, we learn to fly.

The journey long, but joy remains,
Each heartbeat sung, in sweet refrains.
In quiet moments, strength is found,
In faithful tones, our souls abound.

The path may twist, and shadows play,
But in our hearts, there's light of day.
As faithful pilgrims, we draw near,
In whispered prayers, we cast our fear.

With every dawn, a chance to rise,
In trust we walk, beneath the skies.
A tapestry of grace we weave,
In every moment, we believe.

So let us walk, with purpose clear,
In faithful tones, we persevere.
For every step, we take in grace,
In unity, we find our place.

Whispers of the Redeemed

In soft tones, our stories blend,
Each whispered prayer, a heart to mend.
Through trials faced, in shadows cast,
We find the light, our fears surpassed.

The cry for mercy, sweetly shared,
In every soul, the love declared.
With grateful hearts, we lift our praise,
In whispers soft, we find our ways.

For every burden, grace abounds,
In love's embrace, redemption sounds.
With hands held high, we claim the truth,
In sacred bonds of joy and youth.

Each whisper holds a story dear,
In every voice, we banish fear.
With faithful hearts, united strong,
In whispers soft, we sing our song.

So let us gather, souls entwined,
In whispered truths, our hearts aligned.
For in the silence, grace will lead,
In whispers of the redeemed, we heed.

Chants of the Morning Light

Awakening dawn, the light breaks free,
Whispers of hope, a soft decree,
In every heart, a sacred song,
We rise with grace, where we belong.

The sun ascends, the shadows flee,
A golden touch on land and sea,
The sky unfolds, a canvas bright,
We gather strength in morning light.

With hands uplifted, we praise the day,
In every breath, we find our way,
Creation's hymn in every breath,
Bringing solace, banishing death.

The birds proclaim, their voices soar,
A chorus rich, forevermore,
In unity, we raise our song,
To the Divine, where we belong.

So let us walk, in sacred stride,
With faith as our eternal guide,
In every step, the path we trace,
Is woven close with love and grace.

Illumination in Every Note

In quietude, the notes arise,
Echoing forth beneath the skies,
A melody that breaks the night,
Illuminating, pure and bright.

Each chord a whisper from above,
Extended hands, a call of love,
In harmony, we find our place,
With every sound, a sacred grace.

The wind carries the song of life,
Dissolving fear, dispelling strife,
A symphony of joy and peace,
In music's arms, our worries cease.

As rivers dance and branches sway,
The universe joins in the play,
In vibrant strings, we are entwined,
Each note a truth, divinely mined.

So let us sing with voices clear,
The song of love, forever near,
In every note, a heart enthroned,
In sacred echoes, we are home.

The Sacred Dance of Creation

Underneath the starry dome,
The cosmos spins, a vibrant home,
In rhythm's flow, creation breathes,
A dance of life, the soul receives.

In every step, the world awake,
A sacred pulse, the earth shall shake,
With fire and water, air and earth,
In union found, we claim our worth.

The moonlight glows, a guiding hand,
Enfolding all across the land,
Our bodies sway to ancient chants,
In movement pure, our spirit dances.

With grace divine, we turn and spin,
In the circle, we are within,
The cycle spins, the seasons change,
Yet love's embrace shall not estrange.

So let us leap, with hearts ablaze,
In the sacred dance, we give our praise,
For in each twirl, our essence sings,
A testament to the joy life brings.

Celestial Vocalization

In twilight's calm, a voice so pure,
Resonates through the shadows' lure,
A lyrical hymn from stars above,
Inviting souls to share their love.

The heavens hum with vibrant light,
Celestial bonds that feel so right,
Within the silence, secrets share,
A sacred truth floats on the air.

With every breath, a prayer ascends,
In unison, the heart transcends,
Our spirits soar, unbound, divine,
In sacred vocalization, we shine.

The angels' chorus fills the night,
An anthem born of pure delight,
In harmony, we weave our fate,
With every note, we celebrate.

So let us call with voices raised,
In the celestial, our souls are praised,
Together we sing, forever whole,
In love's embrace, we find our role.

Celestial Rhapsody

In the heavens bright and vast,
Wonders sing from ages past.
Stars like candles in the night,
Guide our souls to holy light.

Whispers of the cosmic breath,
Life transcends the shadowed death.
Every note, a prayer set free,
In the dance of eternity.

Angelic voices fill the air,
Harmonies beyond compare.
Every heartbeat, every sigh,
An echo of the sacred sky.

In the silence, wisdom lies,
Hearts uplifted, voices rise.
With each pulse, a world reborn,
In the love that every dawn.

Join the rapture, feel the grace,
In the vast and endless space.
Together, we shall always find,
Celestial rhapsody aligned.

A Reverent Return to Harmony

In the meadow, whispers grow,
Nature's grace begins to flow.
Every leaf, a sacred song,
Guiding us where we belong.

With each footstep on the ground,
Faith in every heart is found.
In the stillness, prayers entwine,
Echoes of the divine design.

Streams of mercy gently weave,
Bringing hope for those who grieve.
In the quilt of life we tread,
Faith revives the hearts once dead.

Lift your gaze and feel the peace,
In the bond that will not cease.
Every moment, a chance to see,
Harmony in you and me.

Join the chorus, be the light,
In the day, or in the night.
With each breath, take part in grace,
A reverent return to place.

The Silent Song of Faith

In the quiet of the heart,
Faith begins, a gentle start.
In still waters, truth resides,
Where the soul in peace abides.

Words unspoken, yet they soar,
In the silence, seek and explore.
Every heartbeat, every tear,
A melody, so soft, yet clear.

In the shadow, light will break,
Every promise, every ache.
In the whispers, hope unfurls,
A silent song that fills the worlds.

With every prayer, a bridge is made,
Uniting all, a serenade.
In the calm, find strength anew,
In faith's embrace, we are true.

Listen closely, feel the call,
In the quiet, lose it all.
Every moment, sacred space,
The silent song of faith's embrace.

Sacred Strings of Existence

From the depths of night we rise,
Plucked by hands of unseen skies.
Every strum, a story told,
In the warmth against the cold.

With each chord that fills the air,
Life's a tapestry we share.
Every note a blissful ring,
Bound by sacred, timeless string.

In the symphony of grace,
All creation finds its place.
With each harmony we sing,
Binds us tight, eternal string.

Feel the pulse of earth and star,
In the stillness, near and far.
Join the dance, let spirits flow,
In the love that we both know.

Let the music ever play,
In our hearts, come what may.
Sacred strings in life persist,
A divine, unbroken tryst.

A Celestial Resurgence

In twilight's grace, the heavens shine,
The stars align, a love divine.
With whispers soft, the angels sing,
A call to hearts, a sacred spring.

The world awakens from its night,
As dawn bestows its gentle light.
In every soul, a flame ignites,
Resurrecting dreams with sheer delight.

With every breath, a promise made,
In faith and hope, we are remade.
Together we shall rise and soar,
To realms of peace forevermore.

O'er mountains high and valleys low,
The sacred river's waters flow.
In every tear, a lesson learned,
Through trials faced, our spirits burned.

Let every heart in chorus sing,
Of love and grace that heaven brings.
In unity, we find our way,
A celestial guide through every day.

The Anthem of Everlasting Light

In shadows deep, a beacon glows,
A light that only wisdom knows.
Through every trial, it shall remain,
A guiding star beyond the pain.

With voices raised in harmony,
We find our strength in unity.
Against the storms, we shall not sway,
For love reveals the safer way.

The tapestry of life unfolds,
In every thread, a story told.
Through joy and sorrow, we shall stand,
In faith's embrace, hand in hand.

A symphony of hope and grace,
In every heart, a sacred space.
As dawn breaks forth, the shadows flee,
The anthem sings, forever free.

With every heartbeat, we shall share,
The light of love in every prayer.
In every moment, pure and bright,
We find our pathway in the light.

Blessed Harmonies of the Soul

In gentle whispers, spirits rise,
To reach the vast and boundless skies.
With every note, a bond is made,
In harmony, our fears allayed.

Each soul a song, unique and true,
Through silent prayers, we are renewed.
With every heartbeat, love does swell,
In sacred rhythms, all is well.

With open arms, we find our peace,
In unity, our joys increase.
Through trials faced, we gather strength,
Together, we will go the length.

In every laugh, a truth revealed,
In every wound, a heart is healed.
The blessed harmonies we sing,
A gift of grace, eternal spring.

Let not despair each heart invade,
For love endures and will not fade.
In sacred bond, we are one whole,
The blessed harmonies of the soul.

Seraphic Songs of the Morning

Awake, O world, to morning's call,
The seraphs sing, inspiring all.
With wings of light, they soar on high,
Their melodies weave through the sky.

Each note a blessing, pure and bright,
In dawn's embrace, a sacred light.
With open hearts, we greet the day,
In gratitude, we find our way.

Through gentle whispers of the breeze,
The spirit moves, our souls at ease.
In every corner, love shall thrive,
With seraphic songs, we come alive.

Let voices blend in sweet refrain,
With every joy, we conquer pain.
In morning's glow, our hopes reborn,
United in the light of dawn.

With every breath, we draw in grace,
In seraphs' song, we find our place.
Together, let our praises rise,
To greet the heavens, free and wise.

The New Symphony of the Soul

In the silence, the spirit sings,
A melody of grace and light.
Harmony rises as heart takes wing,
Transforming shadows into bright.

Each note a message from above,
Hope weaves through every chord.
Faith dances in rhythms of love,
A symphony, our hearts restored.

The pulse of creation, a sacred beat,
Echoing deep in every soul.
In unity, we find our seat,
Together, we make the holy whole.

In the symphony, we yield and blend,
The sacred as we intertwine.
Life's journey, a song without end,
In every heart, divine design.

So let us rise, in voices clear,
Embrace the music's radiant call.
In the vastness, we conquer fear,
The new symphony unites us all.

God's Whisper in the Winds of Change

In the breeze, a gentle sigh,
A whisper laced with grace and care.
Trust the winds when spirits fly,
Guiding hearts to realms more fair.

From shadows deep, new paths will bloom,
Each gust, a promise of the dawn.
In every storm, dispelling gloom,
God's voice, the light that beckons on.

When doubt entangles the heart's sweet song,
Listen closely to the air's sweet plea.
The winds will carry you along,
In God's embrace, you're truly free.

Change is life, a sacred flow,
A dance with destiny, embrace the song.
In God's whisper, blessings grow,
And in surrender, you belong.

So fear not, for the winds will lead,
To pastures lush and skies of blue.
In every heartbeat, plant the seed,
Of faith and love, forever true.

Seraphim's Lullaby of New Beginnings

In the night, the angels sing,
Soft voices cradle dreams anew.
Seraphim's gifts, in crystal ring,
A lullaby that brings hope through.

With every note, the dawn awakes,
Golden light spills from the skies.
In their song, the heart remakes,
In gentle whispers, spirit flies.

New beginnings, upon the breeze,
In the shadows, light takes form.
Seraphim's grace, our souls appease,
Wrapped in love, forever warm.

As stars align and worlds unite,
The lullaby weaves dreams entwined.
In every heart, the spark ignites,
A gift of love, divinely designed.

So rest now, child, in peace and grace,
Let seraphim guard your sleep tight.
In every heartbeat, time and space,
New beginnings glow with holy light.

Whispers from the Celestial Choir

Heaven's song, a fragile thread,
Carried on the wings of night.
With every note, our spirits spread,
In harmony, we seek the light.

From realms divine, the whispers beam,
A call to hearts that yearn for peace.
In reverie, we weave the dream,
Embraced by love that will not cease.

In the quiet, a chorus swells,
Voices blend in sacred play.
In the light, the mystery dwells,
Guiding us along the way.

So lift your soul, let the music soar,
The choir beckons from above.
United, we are evermore,
In the light of everlasting love.

With every breath, we join the song,
In celestial notes, our spirits rise.
In unity, together strong,
We'll find the truth beyond the skies.

Chimes of the Spirit's Call

In the silence, whispers soar,
Echoes of love, forevermore.
Gentle breezes, voices mild,
The heart of heaven, pure and wild.

Chiming bells, a soft refrain,
Awakening hope, calming pain.
Every toll a sacred sign,
Drawing souls to love divine.

In the twilight, light descends,
Guiding paths where faith extends.
Through the shadows, light will gleam,
Comfort found in every dream.

Lift your spirits, let them rise,
In gratitude, hear the cries.
Join the chorus, voices blend,
In this journey, hearts will mend.

Chimes will fade, but still they'll sing,
Eternal truths that love will bring.
In each moment, grace will dwell,
Hearts united, all is well.

Melodic Journeys Toward Grace

On winding roads, we seek His face,
Every step, a dance of grace.
Through valleys deep and mountains high,
With faith as wings, we learn to fly.

Whispers soft as morning dew,
Lead us onward, fresh and new.
In the quiet, find our song,
Melodies to which we belong.

Hearts in rhythm, hands held tight,
Together we embrace the light.
In the stillness, truth will rise,
Opening to the endless skies.

Each note a prayer, each breath a vow,
In sacred moments, listen now.
Along this path, where love prevails,
Unity in gentle trails.

Let our spirits dance and twirl,
In the grace of love, we whirl.
As one we journey, side by side,
In the arms of faith, we bide.

The Seraphic Strain

Above the world, seraphs sing,
In celestial light, their praises ring.
Wings of glory, bright and fair,
Carrying hopes upon the air.

With joyful hearts, they raise their song,
Inviting all to come along.
Heaven's harmony, sweet and pure,
In each verse, we find our cure.

Through trials fierce and storms that roar,
The seraphic strain opens doors.
In every challenge, grace will flow,
As we trust in the love we know.

In the heavens, voices blend,
Traces of a love without end.
Healing whispers in the night,
Fill the soul with sheer delight.

Angelic choruses, forever bright,
Guide our spirits toward the light.
In every note, a sacred dream,
United in the seraph's theme.

Songs of the Abiding Faith

In the garden where we pray,
Songs of faith pave the way.
Each petal sings a gentle truth,
In the heart, eternal youth.

First light breaks, a new day born,
Promises kept, our spirits worn.
Hope awakens, rises strong,
In His arms, we all belong.

With every hymn that lifts our gaze,
We find our peace, our hearts ablaze.
In the joy, a quiet grace,
Carried forth in love's embrace.

Faith like rivers, flowing free,
Washes over, setting free.
Every trial, a lesson learned,
In the flames, our souls are turned.

Songs of hope shall ever rise,
In the darkness, find the skies.
With each note, we sing and stand,
Hand in hand, as He planned.

The Songbird's Lament of Hope

In the stillness of dawn, she sings,
A melody of faith that softly clings.
Through shadows deep, her voice will soar,
A song of hope forevermore.

With every note, the heart takes flight,
As whispers of love break the night.
Each fleeting moment, a sacred chance,
To dance with grace in joyful prance.

Beneath the weight of trials faced,
Her spirit shines, unbent, embraced.
In darkest hours, she finds her way,
A beacon bright, a guiding ray.

Though storms may rage and fears arise,
Her song ascends, a sweet surprise.
In nature's choir, she finds her place,
Resilient heart, draped in grace.

So let us listen, hearts attune,
To the songbird's sweet and gentle tune.
For in her lament, we too will rise,
In faith's embrace, beneath the skies.

The Serene Cadence of Belief

In tranquil whispers, faith unfolds,
A serene cadence, like stories told.
With hands uplifted, souls align,
In sacred unity, divinely designed.

Each heartbeat echoes, a prayer sincere,
Reviving hopes, dispelling fear.
In every breath, communion found,
With sacred love that knows no bound.

In the quiet moments, grace flows free,
A gentle nudge, a light we see.
With every step, on this path we tread,
Faith like a river, forever fed.

Through trials faced, through joy and pain,
The cadence lingers, a sweet refrain.
Together as one, we journey on,
With hearts ignited, the light of dawn.

So let us cherish this blessed way,
In serene cadence, we humbly sway.
For in our belief, we find the key,
Unlocking doors to eternity.

The Harmonious Call to Renewal

Awaken, soul, to the morning light,
A harmonious call, pure and bright.
In every dawn, a chance reborn,
To rise anew, like the golden morn.

With spirits lifted, hope ignites,
The promise of change in tranquil sights.
Each heartbeat a rhythm, strong and true,
In this symphony, we are renewed.

Let nature sing and guide our way,
In gentle whispers, day by day.
From shadows cast, to brighter skies,
In the grace of love, our spirit flies.

Through moments cherished, and trials faced,
The call to renewal, beautifully paced.
Together we march, hand in hand,
In faith's embrace, a promised land.

So heed the call that stirs the soul,
With every note, we become whole.
In harmony's song, we find our place,
In the dance of life, a sacred grace.

Chorus of the Faithful Journey

In the chorus of life, we walk as one,
Bound by love under the rising sun.
Through valleys low and mountains high,
In faith we journey, on wings we fly.

With every step, our voices blend,
In unity strong, as we ascend.
With hearts entwined, we face the night,
Together we stand, ever in light.

In trials faced, our spirits rise,
In the faithful chorus, hope never dies.
Each note a testament of grace,
In shared belief, we find our place.

Through joy and sorrow, laughter and tears,
We sing our truth, dispelling fears.
From different paths, we gather near,
In faith's embrace, we persevere.

So let us raise our voices high,
As humble servants, we reach for the sky.
In the chorus of life's grand design,
Together we shine, in love divine.

The Resplendent Melody of Redemption

In shadows deep, His voice does call,
A whisper sweet, embracing all.
With open hearts, we rise anew,
In grace's glow, our spirits brew.

From ashes, hope begins to soar,
Each note of love, we can't ignore.
Forgiveness blooms, a fragrant feast,
In our brokenness, we are released.

The path of light, so brightly shines,
Guided by faith, in love we find.
Through trials faced, our souls unite,
In harmony, we seek the light.

With every prayer, the heavens sing,
A symphony of grace we bring.
In joy and peace, we freely dwell,
The resplendent tale of Him we tell.

Let hearts be stirred, let voices raise,
In holy rhythm, sing His praise.
For in redemption, we are whole,
A melody that heals the soul.

A Choir of New Horizons

Together we stand, a sacred band,
Underneath the skies so grand.
Voices lifted, spirits soar,
Open hearts and so much more.

With every note, we find our way,
Towards the dawn of a brighter day.
Each harmony a path divine,
In unity, our souls align.

Through valleys low and mountains high,
We walk with faith, reaching the sky.
A choir sings of love, so true,
In every heart, His grace imbues.

The horizon calls, a promise near,
In every tear, He wipes our fear.
With open arms, He welcomes home,
In sacred trust, we freely roam.

Let voices rise, let praises flow,
In His embrace, our spirits glow.
Together we rise, through trials we tread,
A choir of hope, where angels led.

Spirit's Tune Reclaimed

In silence bright, a whisper stirs,
The spirit's call, through earthly blurs.
A sacred sound, reclaiming grace,
In every heart, we find our place.

With hands held high, we dance as one,
The battle fought, the victory won.
In melodies pure, we rise anew,
His love, our guide, forever true.

Life's winding path, with sorrow lined,
Yet in His arms, our peace we find.
The spirit's song, a beacon's light,
Guides us through the darkest night.

Each breath we take, a hymn of praise,
In every trial, our faith we raise.
Through pain and joy, His will be done,
The spirit's tune, our hearts as one.

Let praises ring, let spirits soar,
In faith we trust, forevermore.
Through every storm, we stand with grace,
In love's embrace, we find our place.

Divine Reflections in Sacred Verse

Reflected light, so pure and bright,
In sacred verse, we find our sight.
Each word a prayer, a truth revealed,
In spirit's grace, our fate is sealed.

From ancient times, the wisdom flows,
In heart and mind, the spirit grows.
Through every line, His presence near,
With open hearts, we cast our fear.

In love divine, we find our way,
Through darkest nights to brighter days.
With faith as guide, we journey forth,
In sacred verse, we find our worth.

Through trials faced, we learn to trust,
In every struggle, rise we must.
A reflection of His endless grace,
In gratitude, we find our place.

Let every hymn, let every prayer,
Speak of the love that we all share.
In sacred verse, our spirits sing,
Divine reflections, a gift He brings.

The Awakening Anthem

In the silence, hear the call,
A whisper echoes through the hall.
Hearts unite in sacred grace,
Awakening light in this holy space.

Arise, O soul, from shadowed dreams,
Bathe in the light of love that gleams.
With every breath, a promise made,
In faith renewed, let doubts fade.

Hands lifted high to skies above,
Embracing all the gifts of love.
Within this moment, pure and bright,
We stand together, hearts ignite.

Voices rise like morning songs,
Harmonizing where the spirit longs.
In unity, our hearts expand,
Transforming lives with love's own hand.

Let us wander on this path,
Guided by light, away from wrath.
In each step, a grace bestowed,
In awakening, our souls are crowed.

Celestial Strings and Heartfelt Prayers

Strings of light strummed by a muse,
Echoing prayers that we infuse.
Melodies reach the heavens high,
As hearts lift wings, they soar and fly.

In every note, a story shared,
A tapestry of love prepared.
With gentle hands, together we play,
Binding our spirits in sweet ballet.

Prayers softly woven in the night,
Illuminate our dreams with light.
Each heartbeat sings a sacred tune,
Awakening hope beneath the moon.

Celestial strings in perfect harmony,
Teach us to dance in unity.
Let faith unite our every strive,
With heartfelt prayers, our souls revive.

In the quiet of the dawn's embrace,
We gather strength, a holy grace.
Through love's sweet song, we remain near,
In celestial chords, we banish fear.

Sacred Verses of Renewal

In the dawn, a voice calls clear,
Renewal whispers, drawing near.
Like rivers flowing, pure and bright,
We shed our burdens, embrace the light.

Each verse a promise, fresh and new,
A journey taken, paths pursued.
In sacred moments, we find our place,
With hearts united, we seek His grace.

Let not the past cloud our way,
In every breath, a brand new day.
Awakening truth, dispelling fears,
In sacred verses, we shed our tears.

Together we rise, hand in hand,
Filling the earth with love so grand.
In unity's strength, we thrive and grow,
In sacred renewal, His light we show.

Grant us the vision to see the right,
To walk in His presence, filled with light.
With every heartbeat, we sing anew,
In sacred verses, He guides us through.

Illuminated Pathways in Song

Upon the paths where shadows play,
Illumined songs light the way.
Each note a step, each chord a sign,
Guiding our souls, both yours and mine.

In twilight's glow, we find our peace,
A promise that will never cease.
With every melody, hearts unite,
Creating hope in darkest night.

Songs of faith upon the breeze,
Lift our spirits, make us free.
In harmony, we break the chains,
Finding freedom where love reigns.

Through trials faced, together we stand,
Singing praises across the land.
Illuminated by love's embrace,
In every heart, we find our place.

Let every soul be filled with song,
As we walk the path, both bold and strong.
With faith our compass, we journey long,
Together, blessed in anthems along.

Harmony of Dawn

In the soft light of early morn,
Awakens the world, a new day born.
Whispers of peace in the gentle breeze,
Guiding our hearts, bringing us ease.

Each leaf dances in radiant glow,
Nature sings prayers, a vibrant show.
Sunrise unveils the promise so bright,
In harmony's arms, we find our light.

Birds take flight with joyous refrain,
Echoes of love in the sweet terrain.
Every heartbeat syncs to the sound,
In this sacred space, grace can be found.

With every color, the sky unfolds,
Stories of life in the sunrise told.
Unity flourishes in morning's embrace,
Together we stand, in joy we trace.

Dawn paints the world with brush of hope,
In the light of faith, we learn to cope.
Together we journey, hand in hand,
In the harmony of the dawn, we stand.

Sacred Chords of Renewal

In every heartbeat, the sacred beat,
Life whispers softly, though the world's fleet.
Chords of renewal fill the sacred space,
Binding us gently, in love's warm embrace.

Through trials faced with strength divine,
We rise above, our spirits align.
Hands raised high, in gratitude sing,
For every blessing that life may bring.

The river flows, cleansing the soul,
Each ripple a note, making us whole.
With faith as our guide, we venture forth,
In this sacred dance, we find our worth.

Under the stars, our dreams take flight,
Each prayer a melody, echoing light.
Together we stand, united in grace,
In sacred chords, we find our place.

Awakened spirits in love's sweet flow,
Blooming anew as our hearts overflow.
In the arms of renewal, we find our song,
In the sacred chords, we always belong.

Voices of the Divine Awakening

Listen closely to the whispers near,
The voices of love, ever sincere.
In the silence, truth begins to rise,
Awakening hearts under vast skies.

Each note a prayer, a soft serenade,
Calling our souls, never to fade.
From the depths of darkness, we emerge,
With voices united, in harmony surge.

Faith shines brightly in the darkened night,
Guiding the weary towards the light.
In the symphony of life, we are one,
Dancing together until the day's done.

The echoes of wisdom fill the air,
Reminding us always to show we care.
In shared moments, divinity's grace,
We rise together, sacred embrace.

Awakening love in the silent still,
Voices of truth, our hearts they fill.
In the divine echo, we find our way,
With every heartbeat, we seek to stay.

Melodies of Grace Unfurled

In the quiet dawn, grace unfolds,
Melodies sweet, as creation holds.
Each gentle breeze carries love's refrain,
A song of hope, washing away pain.

With every heartbeat, a symphony swells,
Stories of light that the spirit tells.
Embracing the moment, we serenade,
In melodious whispers, our fears fade.

The stars above, they twinkle and shine,
Guided by faith, a path so divine.
In the dance of life, we are intertwined,
Melodies weaving, the sacred aligned.

With open hearts, we gather as one,
In harmonies sweet, our souls begun.
Sharing the joy that the spirit brings,
In the melodies of grace, our love sings.

As shadows retreat, we rise anew,
In the light of grace, our spirits grew.
Together we flourish, in this joyful world,
In the beauty of love, our hopes unfurled.

The Spirit's Verse

In whispers soft, the Spirit calls,
Through shadowed paths, where silence sprawls.
A guiding light, in darkest night,
Awakening souls, with holy might.

Each tear we shed, a sacred prayer,
In valleys deep, His love we share.
Through trials faced, we rise anew,
In faith's embrace, there's nothing we can't do.

A harmony of hearts, entwined as one,
With every breath, our journey's begun.
Beneath the stars, we find our way,
In the presence of grace, we choose to stay.

Let voices blend, in joyful praise,
For grace abounds in endless ways.
Lift up our hands, surrendering hope,
We walk together, through love we cope.

A spirit's dance, a sacred lace,
In every moment, we seek His face.
With open hearts, the truth we find,
In the Spirit's verse, we are aligned.

Hymn of Deliverance

From chains unbound, we call His name,
In shadows cast, He'll fan the flame.
With each refrain, our spirits soar,
In love's embrace, we are restored.

Through trials fierce, His light breaks through,
Deliverance found, the heart made new.
With every step, we walk in grace,
And darkness fades, we seek His face.

The broken cry, for mercy's hand,
A promise given, we understand.
In joyous songs, our hearts align,
For in His peace, our souls entwine.

Together we rise, our voices clear,
A hymn of hope for all who hear.
With faith as our shield, we share His love,
In unity strong, we rise above.

In every struggle, we find the way,
With open hearts, we humbly pray.
Deliverance comes, a heavenly sign,
In the hymn of grace, our souls combine.

Nocturnal Reveries of the Divine

Beneath the stars, in silent night,
The heart takes wing, in sacred flight.
With every sigh, the spirits breathe,
In twilight's hush, we find reprieve.

The moonlight beams, a guiding hand,
In darkness deep, we understand.
A tapestry of dreams unfolds,
As whispered prayers in silence hold.

In reverie's grasp, we seek His grace,
A tranquil peace, in this holy space.
With faith ignited, we trust the way,
In the night's embrace, our fears allay.

With gentle hearts, we listen near,
For sacred truths, His voice we hear.
In every shadow, hope ignites,
Through nocturnal dreams, we seek the light.

As dawn approaches, the night shall wane,
In every loss, there is a gain.
In reveries divine, we find our song,
With love beside us, we shall belong.

God's Great Symphony

In every heartbeat, a note resounds,
The symphony of life, where love abounds.
With every breath, the music plays,
A melody of grace through all our days.

The strings of hope vibrate in tune,
In harmony found beneath the moon.
With gentle hands, we shape the sound,
As joy and sorrow in love are bound.

Each trial faced, a chord we make,
A canvas bright, for life's sweet sake.
In rhythms sweet, our spirits blend,
Through storms endured, we find a friend.

Together we soar, in one refrain,
Through valleys low and mountains' gain.
In God's great symphony, we unite,
With hearts ablaze, we share the light.

As echoes fade, we carry on,
In every dawn, a new love's song.
With faith's embrace, our hearts ignite,
In God's great symphony, we find our might.

Dawn's Harmonious Offering

In whispers soft, the sun ascends,
Awakening the world with grace,
Each ray a prayer, each hue transcends,
Embracing all in warm embrace.

The golden light breaks night's still bind,
A symphony of hope unspun,
In every heart, new peace to find,
As day begins, our souls are one.

The trees, they sway, a dance divine,
With rustling leaves, their voices rise,
In harmony, their roots entwine,
A chorus sweet beneath the skies.

The rivers sing, the mountains hum,
Creation's song in every part,
As nature's choir makes welcome,
The dawning love within each heart.

Let us join in this sacred tune,
With open arms and lifted eyes,
For in each dawn, God's love renews,
A gift bestowed, a sweet reprise.

The Sacred Dialogue of Nature's Voice

Beneath the boughs where shadows dwell,
A murmuring brook begins to flow,
It speaks of peace, of love's soft swell,
In nature's heart, wisdom does grow.

The mountains stand in silent prayer,
Their heights a testament of grace,
In every stone, a tale laid bare,
Of ancient whispers time can't erase.

The wind, it carries sacred lore,
With every breath, the Spirit calls,
In rustling leaves, a gentle score,
Where echoes weave through nature's halls.

Each flower blooms, a prayer in hue,
Colors burst forth in joyous light,
Nature's canvas, pure and true,
Reflecting love in day and night.

Thus let us heed the sacred sound,
In every glimpse of earth we see,
For in this dialogue profound,
We find the roots of unity.

Celestial Reflections in the Stillness

In silent nights, the stars awake,
Their light a map of dreams untold,
In tranquil skies, the heavens quake,
With mysteries wrapped in silver fold.

The moon, a lantern high above,
Illuminates the soul's deep quest,
In its embrace, we find our love,
A mirror soft, where hearts find rest.

The breeze whispers secrets of grace,
As shadows dance upon the ground,
In every pause, we seek His face,
In stillness, sacred truths abound.

Reflections in the dark unite,
Awakening the stars' soft glow,
In every heart, a flicker bright,
A glimpse of love in cosmic flow.

So let us gaze beyond the night,
And find in silence God's embrace,
For in these moments pure delight,
Celestial blessings we can trace.

The Beat of the Eternal Heart

In every heartbeat, life does pulse,
A rhythm known to all who breathe,
A testament of love, convulse,
In every moment, we believe.

The world awakes with morning's grace,
Each heartbeat echoes joy, sublime,
A dance of souls in time and space,
Connecting all, beyond all time.

The sacred beat, it calls us near,
With lifeblood flowing through the land,
In every joy, in every tear,
A unity we cannot strand.

The music of the heart resounds,
In laughter shared, in sorrow's song,
For in this love, hope abounds,
Together whole, we all belong.

So let our hearts align and sing,
To honor life, the gift we share,
For in each beat, a sacred ring,
A promise made, a faithful prayer.

The Sacred Conductor's Baton

In the stillness, hear the call,
A baton raised, the echoes fall.
With gentle hands, align the song,
Where hearts unite, we all belong.

Notes of peace, a rhythm pure,
Each soul's purpose, to endure.
Harmony in diverse array,
Guides us through the darkest day.

In sacred time, we find our grace,
The Conductor lifts, in love embrace.
Together we weave a symphony,
In every note, a unity.

Let the cadence shape the light,
In shadows, bring forth joy's delight.
With every beat, a prayer ascends,
The sacred call that never ends.

So raise your voice, let spirits soar,
With each refrain, we seek for more.
The fabric strong, through trials span,
In faith we stand, a timeless plan.

Weaving Melodies of Compassion

In gentle hands, the heartstrings pull,
Each note a tear, each chord a lull.
Weaving warmth through every sound,
Compassion blooms where love is found.

The echoes rise, a soft embrace,
In sacred harmony, we find our place.
Every sorrow, each joy intertwined,
In music's arms, true peace combined.

Listen close, the whispers call,
From mountain high to valley's fall.
With every strum, let kindness flow,
In the melody, let compassion grow.

Serenade the weary soul,
In laughter and in tears, make whole.
A tapestry of sound divine,
Where every heart and spirit shine.

Let the rhythms heal and mend,
In every note, a love to lend.
With dulcet tones, our spirits dance,
In life's embrace, we take a chance.

An Offering of Divine Chords

Upon the altar, let us lay,
An offering of chord and sway.
Strum the heartstrings, play the part,
To honor every sacred heart.

In harmony, our voices blend,
With gratitude, our spirits send.
From depths of soul, the praises rise,
A sweet surrender to the skies.

With open arms, we take the leap,
In divine music, solace deep.
Each chord a step, each note a prayer,
In every breath, pure love we share.

Let joy resound in colors bright,
Within the shadows, bring the light.
In every strum, a grace bestowed,
A pathway bright where hope has flowed.

Together we sing, a sacred song,
In unity, we all belong.
An offering of love outpoured,
In divine chords, our spirits soared.

Light's Everlasting Praise

In the dawn, when shadows fade,
Light emerges, blessings laid.
With every ray, a voice resounds,
In light's embrace, true joy abounds.

Let praises rise with morning dew,
In every heart, a vision new.
For in the light, darkness departs,
Each beam of love to mend our hearts.

With every glance, and every smile,
Reflecting grace, we walk the mile.
With arms wide open, we receive,
In the glow, we learn to believe.

Sing unto the stars above,
In every twinkle, shines His love.
With notes of faith, and hymns of peace,
In light's embrace, may troubles cease.

So let us gather, hand in hand,
In light's embrace, we take our stand.
With everlasting praise we sing,
In truth and love, hope's offering.

Hymns of the Resurrected Heart

In shadows deep, the light breaks through,
Hearts awakened, souls anew.
With fervent praise we lift our voice,
In gratitude, we make our choice.

From ashes rise, the spirit sings,
A melody of sacred things.
With every step, our faith we share,
Together bound in love and care.

The risen dawn, a hope restored,
In every moment, He's adored.
In silence, find His gentle hand,
A guiding grace through every land.

With joy we march, unyielding hearts,
In every life, His love imparts.
To every soul, a beacon bright,
Our faith unfolds, a wondrous sight.

So here we stand, united strong,
In harmony, we sing our song.
For in His arms, we find our worth,
A hymn of peace upon the earth.

Echoes of Celestial Whispers

In quiet night, the stars proclaim,
The whispers soft call out His name.
With every breath, we hear His grace,
In sacred space, we find our place.

The moonlight dances, shadows fade,
In every heart, His love displayed.
We close our eyes and seek the light,
In evening's glow, all fears take flight.

O gentle breeze, His touch divine,
In nature's hymn, our spirits align.
With faith, we wander, hand in hand,
Through valleys deep and golden sand.

His voice, a fountain, pure and clear,
In every joy, we hold Him near.
With tender hope, our souls unite,
In echoes soft, we find His light.

A symphony of love unfolds,
In every heart, His story told.
With grateful hearts, we rise and sing,
In every dawn, His blessings bring.

The Symphony of Hope Resounds

In every heart, a song begins,
A symphony of grace within.
With every chord, our spirits swell,
In unity, His love we tell.

Through trials faced, we find our voice,
In every tear, we make a choice.
To rise again, to stand in light,
A testament to hope's pure sight.

The rhythms of the world may clash,
But in His peace, our fears abash.
With steadfast hearts, we walk this path,
Embracing joy, dispelling wrath.

In whispers soft, His truth prevails,
Through stormy seas and gentle gales.
With every breath, we strive to see,
The beauty of His harmony.

Together, we shall lift our hands,
In praise, we meet, where love expands.
For in this life, hope's song resounds,
In every heart, His grace abounds.

Psalms of Transformative Light

In darkest nights, His truth shall shine,
With every step, our hearts align.
From shadowed paths, to radiant days,
His light transforms, our spirits praise.

With faith renewed, we journey forth,
In every trial, we find our worth.
A beacon bright in stormy skies,
With open hearts, the spirit flies.

In gentle dawn, the world awakes,
His mercy flows, the heart it makes.
In every laugh, in every tear,
His love surrounds, dispelling fear.

We gather close, in sacred prayer,
In every heartbeat, we declare.
For in our lives, His strength we find,
A transformative love, truly kind.

Through every moment, hope ignites,
In unity, we share the light.
With joyous hymn, we sing our part,
Psalms of light from every heart.

Songs Born from Suffering

In shadows deep, where burdens lie,
Voices rise like wings to fly.
Through tears that fall, a melody,
Whispers of strength, setting us free.

A heart once bruised, now beats in grace,
Each scar a tale, each wound a trace.
Through trials faced, the soul will grow,
In darkest night, a light will glow.

With heavy hearts, we gather near,
In unity found, we conquer fear.
The chorus swells, a sacred song,
Reminding us where we belong.

O'er mountains high and valleys low,
Faith blooms in whispers, soft and slow.
With every note, our spirits soar,
In suffering, love finds its core.

So let us sing, through pain and strife,
For songs of hope are born from life.
In every struggle, grace will gleam,
The heart's true song, a precious dream.

A Tapestry of Faithful Voices

Threads of spirit weave our way,
In unity, we choose to stay.
Each story told, a cherished part,
Stitching love within the heart.

In every voice, a tale of trust,
From ashes rise, in faith we must.
A tapestry of woven light,
Guides us through the darkest night.

With hands held tight, we stand as one,
In shared belief, our race is run.
The fabric strong, though frayed by sin,
In every loss, there's strength within.

A song of joy, a hymn of peace,
In faithful bonds, our fears release.
Together we tread this holy ground,
In every heartbeat, love is found.

So let us gather, voices raise,
In harmony, our spirits blaze.
A tapestry, rich and bold,
In every thread, the love we hold.

The Harmonious Call of Spirit

In quiet hours when shadows fall,
A whisper sweet, the spirit's call.
It beckons forth through nights so long,
A sacred hymn, a heart's pure song.

With every breath, divinity near,
In gentle winds, the truth is clear.
We walk together, hand in hand,
In faithful steps, we understand.

Through trials faced, the spirit speaks,
In gentle tones, through strong and weak.
Each moment shared, a blessing shared,
In loving grace, we're always paired.

The music swells, a joyous ring,
A melody that life will bring.
In every soul, the echoes blend,
A harmony that will not end.

So rise, dear hearts, to meet the day,
Embrace the light, let spirits play.
In sacred trust, our voices soar,
The harmonious call forevermore.

Chords of Hope and Redemption

Within the strife, a note resounds,
In chords of hope, our faith abounds.
Each trial faced, a lesson learned,
From ashes rise, our hearts are burned.

In moments lost, redemption waits,
A melody that love creates.
Through darkest days, we find the light,
In every struggle, we take flight.

With every chord, the spirit sweeps,
A promise made, a love that keeps.
In shared belief, we lift our gaze,
In harmony, we sing His praise.

In joy and sorrow, hand in hand,
In every heart, the truth will stand.
The song of hope, a sacred climb,
In perfect rhythm, transcending time.

So let us play this vibrant tune,
A song resplendent, like the moon.
In chords of grace, we find our way,
Redemption's light leads us today.

Harmonious Tributes to the Divine

In silence we gather, hearts align,
Lifting our voices, sacred and fine.
With each gentle breath, we send our prayer,
To the heights above, love fills the air.

Through valleys we wander, guided by light,
In shadows we find, the spark shining bright.
Each moment a gift, each star a sign,
In all of creation, the divine we find.

With hands gently clasped, we seek to share,
The beauty of love, a bond so rare.
In kindness we gather, hearts intertwined,
In every act of grace, the divine defined.

In the warmth of the sun, we feel the embrace,
A tapestry woven, each thread a trace.
With every soft whisper, with every glance,
We dance in the presence, a holy romance.

So let us be humble, let hearts unfold,
In the stories of life, let our spirits be bold.
With tributes of love, we rise and we sing,
United in purpose, a celestial ring.

The Dance of Joyful Praise

In the morning light, we dance and we sing,
With spirits uplifted, joy is our wing.
Every heartbeat echoes, a rhythm divine,
In the warmth of grace, our souls intertwine.

With every step taken, we honor the call,
To cherish each moment, to rise, never fall.
In laughter and love, we find our pure way,
In the glow of the dawn, our hearts brightly sway.

From the mountains high to the rivers that flow,
We gather together, with hearts all aglow.
In harmony lifted, our voices will blend,
In the dance of devotion, we shall never end.

With hands raised to heaven, we celebrate life,
In the joy of the spirit, we conquer all strife.
In unity shining, we share our embrace,
In the dance of love, we find sacred space.

So let us rejoice in the rhythm of grace,
In the dance of existence, we find our true place.
With every sweet act, every deed we adorn,
In the dance of our praise, a new world is born.

An Invocation in Every Note

In melodies woven, our hearts take flight,
Each note a soft echo, of love and of light.
In sacred vibrations, our spirits arise,
An invocation whispered, beneath open skies.

With instruments played, and voices so pure,
We seek the connection, a bond that is sure.
Through valleys and peaks, our song shall resound,
In the depths of our being, the sacred is found.

Each chord brings us closer, to realms yet unseen,
In the music of ages, where hearts have been keen.
A tapestry formed, with threads of delight,
In the harmony offered, we find our true sight.

Let joy be our anthem, let peace lead the way,
In each heartfelt chorus, let love guide our stay.
In the beauty of sound, we'll forever take flight,
An invocation of grace, both day and night.

So join in the chorus, let spirits unite,
With every note strummed, bring darkness to light.
In the symphony crafted, let love always flow,
An invocation eternal, a gift we bestow.

The Serene Whisper of Grace

In the hush of the morning, where stillness resides,
A whisper of grace, on gentle winds glides.
With every soft breath, the world finds its peace,
In the calmness embraced, all troubles may cease.

Through gardens of hope, where the spirit can roam,
In each flower's song, we find our way home.
With every soft rustle, each leaf's tender sway,
The serene whisper calls, guiding the way.

In the twilight's glow, where shadows retreat,
The echo of love, in our hearts, we keep.
With the stars as our lanterns, we journey anew,
In the gentle caress, we discover the true.

With faith as our anchor, our prayers rise high,
In the silence of night, we lift up our cry.
In the presence of grace, our sorrows will fade,
In the cradle of mercy, our hearts are remade.

So let us be still, and listen in trust,
To the serene whispers, they guide us, they must.
With open hearts yearning, let love take its place,
In the quiet of moments, we find our own grace.

Voices of Dawn's Embrace

In the hush of morning light,
Whispers of hope take flight.
Hearts aligned with sacred grace,
Embrace the dawn, a holy space.

With each ray that softly glows,
Faith within us gently flows.
Nature sings a vibrant tune,
Awakening the spirit's boon.

Rising sun in skies so clear,
Chasing shadows, banishing fear.
Together in this endless quest,
We find the peace, our hearts' true rest.

In tranquil moments, prayers rise,
To the heavens, the infinite skies.
A chorus of love we now proclaim,
United souls, we call Your name.

Thus, we greet each day divine,
In sacred bonds, our lives entwine.
Voices echo, a timeless song,
In dawn's embrace, where we belong.

Hymns of the Awakening Heart

Softly now the hymns arise,
Awakening hearts to sacred ties.
In silence deep, we hear the call,
A gentle whisper, love for all.

Each note a promise, pure and bright,
Illuminating paths of light.
With every tear, a cleansing grace,
In valleys low, we find our place.

Step by step, the journey unfolds,
With stories woven, truths retold.
Lifted voices, raising high,
Echoes of praise, a joyful sigh.

In the gathering, we find our peace,
A sacred bond that will not cease.
Together we dance, in spirit and time,
Hymns of love in perfect rhyme.

Hear the cadence of hearts in tune,
Under the watchful, guiding moon.
In awakening, we share a part,
A beautiful hymn of the awakening heart.

Serenade of the Soul's Renewal

Softly flows the river's song,
In the heart where we belong.
Beneath the stars, the night so still,
We find the peace, our spirits fill.

Each rustling leaf, a whispered prayer,
With every breath, we feel You near.
In sacred spaces, we find our way,
Embraced by love that will not sway.

Fleeting moments, forever held,
In the warmth of love compelled.
From darkness grows the light within,
The serenade of souls begin.

With open hearts, we cherish grace,
In each renewal, Your sweet embrace.
Journey forth, unbound and free,
In the serenade of unity.

Together, we will rise anew,
In harmony, we shall pursue.
A symphony of life's designs,
In the soul's renewal, love defines.

Echoes of Divine Melodies

In the stillness, echoes sound,
Divine melodies all around.
Each note a thread of sacred lore,
Binding us forevermore.

As the skies spill radiant light,
We hear the whispers of the night.
Songs of heaven, hearts entwined,
In the echoes, solace we find.

Through valleys deep and mountains high,
Melodies of faith we cannot deny.
In every rhythm, a pulse divine,
Guiding us towards the sacred line.

Let the music of love abound,
In every heart, let joy resound.
With arms wide open, we embrace,
The echoes of Your endless grace.

In the journey of the soul's flight,
We sing together through the night.
Echoes of love, forever shared,
In divine melodies, we are bared.

Aria of the Faithful

In whispers low, the faithful pray,
Hearts uplifted, night to day.
A holy hymn in twilight's grace,
Guides the lost to Heaven's place.

With every tear, an angel's song,
In trials faced, we do belong.
Together strong, our spirits rise,
In unity, we claim the skies.

Beneath the stars, in silent nights,
We find our peace, eternal lights.
With trust, we walk the narrow path,
Our souls reborn in love's sweet bath.

A gentle hand, the shepherd's call,
In shadows deep, we shall not fall.
For in His name, we stand as one,
In faith we find, the victory won.

Each prayer a note in sacred air,
Hearts entwined, a bond we share.
In fervent hope, our spirits blend,
In harmony, the soul's defend.

The Divine Lyric

From mountains high, the echoes flow,
In every heart, the praises grow.
With gentle hands, the heavens write,
A symphony that brings delight.

The morning sun, a sacred sign,
In every dawn, His love divine.
We gather close, in grace we dwell,
Each story told, a living well.

A melody of faith resounds,
In every soul, His love abounds.
With every breath, we sing His choir,
In depths of night, igniting fire.

With verses spun from truth and light,
In darkest hours, we find our sight.
Our voices raised, the heavens near,
In joy we share, we banish fear.

Each moment felt, a gift we take,
In love we soar, our spirits wake.
For in this bond, our hearts ignite,
The divine song, our guiding light.

Prayers in the Key of Life

In stillness found, our prayers arise,
A sacred chant beneath the skies.
With faith as strong as mountain stone,
We cast our cares, we are not alone.

In every struggle, strength unfolds,
As love surrounds, and hope retold.
With hearts aglow, we lift our plea,
In harmony, we're truly free.

A testament to grace bestowed,
In trials faced, our spirits road.
With every step, the path revealed,
In prayer, our wounds are healed.

In unity, our voices blend,
Each humble heart, our souls commend.
As stars above bear witness true,
In faith, we rise, anew, anew.

Our prayers, like rivers, gently flow,
A bond of hope that helps us grow.
For in this key, we learn to sing,
In love's embrace, eternal spring.

Melodies of the Blessed

In sacred woods, the spirits roam,
In every heart, we find a home.
With whispers soft, the breezes dance,
Each note a hymn, a holy chance.

Beneath the arch of azure skies,
In mortal frames, our spirits rise.
With every smile, a spark divine,
In laughter shared, His love we find.

From silence deep, we lift our song,
In every breath, we all belong.
Together blessed, we journey forth,
In faith, we seek our truest worth.

In twilight's glow, the shadows fade,
Our souls reflect the love conveyed.
With gratitude, our hearts express,
In life's embrace, we find our rest.

For every dawn, a chance to rise,
In grace we stand, our voices wise.
In every melody, pure and bright,
We sing together, hearts alight.

The Radiant Resonance of Creation

In the stillness of dawn's embrace,
Light whispers secrets of grace.
Stars awaken, in chorus they sing,
Echoes of love from Creator's wing.

Mountains bow low, rivers rejoice,
Nature's heart beats with one voice.
Petals unfurl in fervent prayer,
A dance of life lingers in the air.

Sky paints hope in colors bold,
Every sunset a story told.
Birdsong rises, a sacred tune,
As day surrenders to the moon.

Hands uplifted, hearts in sync,
In every heartbeat, we drink.
Creation's pulse forever flows,
In each moment, love only grows.

Through the veil of time, we tread,
In the light where we are led.
The universe spins, a dance sublime,
In the radiant resonance of time.

Evensong of Divine Manifestation

As twilight wraps the world in gold,
A symphony of stories unfolds.
Every shadow tells of grace,
In the night, we find our place.

Candles flicker, souls ignite,
In the darkness, we find light.
Voices lifted, prayers ascend,
In evensong, hearts will blend.

Whispers of wisdom in the breeze,
All creation bends its knees.
Stars bear witness to the sacred,
In the moment, faith is awakened.

The gentle night hums a tune,
A lullaby beneath the moon.
In every heart, a spark divine,
In unity, we intertwine.

Life's tapestry, vibrant and wide,
Flowing with love, we abide.
In the embrace of evening's sigh,
We find our truth, together we fly.

Celestial Overture of Change

With the dawn of a new day's breath,
Change awakens, conquering death.
Winds of fate dance through the skies,
In the celestial, spirit flies.

Each moment beckons with its flair,
To bloom anew in the open air.
Mountains shift and rivers bend,
In every ending, we ascend.

Fleeting shadows teach us grace,
In the trials, a holy space.
Stars aligned, whispers of fate,
In change, we become, we create.

Hearts surrender to the flow,
From embers rise, a sacred glow.
In the crucible, pure souls forge,
Transforming paths as we emerge.

In the harmony of life's grand song,
Together we rise, where we belong.
A journey wrapped in love's embrace,
In every heartbeat, we find our place.

Reverent Notes of Transformational Truth

In the silence, truth does dwell,
In every heart, a sacred well.
Words unspoken, wisdom calls,
To rise together, never fall.

Echoes of love in the space between,
A tapestry woven, unseen.
Every heartbeat, a step divine,
In the journey, we intertwine.

Awakening souls, a gentle nudge,
In the stillness, we refuse to budge.
Lessons learned in fear's bright light,
Transforming shadows into sight.

Reverent notes in the voice of the night,
Guide us onward, towards the light.
In distress, find strength anew,
A transformational truth rings true.

As the dawn breaks, hope will rise,
In every heart, the spirit flies.
Together we weave this sacred song,
In the dance of truth, we all belong.

Light's Divine Cadence

In shadows deep, His light shall shine,
A dance of grace, a love divine.
With whispers soft, He calls my name,
In faith I stand, forever same.

Upon the path where angels tread,
In every tear, His love is spread.
Through trials faced, I find my way,
Each moment brightens, come what may.

With every step, my heart will sing,
In praise of Him, my guiding king.
The melody of peace unfolds,
In simple truths, His love consoles.

A journey blessed, and Spirit led,
In every word that He has said.
With open arms, He welcomes me,
In light's embrace, I'm truly free.

From dawn to dusk, His cadence plays,
In every heart, His song will stays.
In harmony, we rise as one,
Together sworn, till day is done.

Celestial Echoes in the Silence

In quiet moments, grace is found,
Celestial echoes, a sacred sound.
As whispers weave through air so pure,
In silence deep, my soul's allure.

Here in the stillness, love takes flight,
A gentle spark in darkest night.
With every breath, the Spirit speaks,
In sacred peace, my heart it seeks.

The stars alight, a divine array,
Guiding my thoughts as I kneel and pray.
In humble reverence, I stand tall,
With faith in Him, I shall not fall.

Each prayer sends ripples through the void,
With every word, the heart enjoyed.
In whispers soft, my hopes arise,
Bathed in the glow of heaven's skies.

A melody of angels sings,
In harmony with all good things.
In trust, I walk, my path made clear,
For in the silence, He is near.

The Instrument of Salvation

In trials faced and burdens borne,
A heart of flesh, from pain is torn.
Yet through the storm, His grace abounds,
In faith renewed, my spirit sounds.

The instrument of my salvation,
In every note, a holy station.
With every chord, His truth arises,
Through love's embrace, the darkness disguises.

In whispered prayers and songs of old,
A story of grace silently told.
The Savior's hand, my guiding light,
In every struggle, He'll win the fight.

With every strife, my hope will bind,
In trusting love, I seek, I find.
Through trials fierce, my soul shall stand,
An instrument in His great plan.

As rivers flow and mountains rise,
In every tear, His mercy lies.
With joy I lift my voice in praise,
For in His light, my heart will blaze.

Threads of Heavenly Harmony

In tapestry of life, we weave,
Threads of hope that never leave.
Each moment stitched with love so bright,
In heavenly harmony, the light.

As seasons change, the fabric grows,
With patterns rich, His mercy flows.
A gathering of hearts aligned,
In unity, our souls entwined.

With gentle hands, the Weaver guides,
Through valleys low and mountains wide.
With every knot, a promise made,
In faith we stand, unafraid.

In joyous songs, our voices blend,
The threads unite, for love won't end.
Through trials faced, we rise and stand,
In every stitch, we find His hand.

With laughter shared and tears embraced,
In this grand design, beauty traced.
For in His grace, we find our way,
Threads of harmony, come what may.

Milton Keynes UK
Ingram Content Group UK Ltd.
UKHW020041271124
451585UK00012B/979